SHOOTING—
WHY WE MISS

SHOOTING— WHY WE MISS

QUESTIONS AND ANSWERS ON THE SUCCESSFUL USE OF THE SHOTGUN

MACDONALD HASTINGS

EDITED FOR U.S.A. BY VIN T. SPARANO
ILLUSTRATED BY TED BURWELL

DAVID McKAY COMPANY, INC.
NEW YORK

Library of Congress Cataloging in Publication Data

Hastings, Macdonald.
  Shooting—why we miss.

  1. Shotguns.   2. Shooting.   3. Fowling.
I. Title.
SK39.H37 1977   799.2′02834   77-8181
ISBN 0-679-50720-5
ISBN 0-679-50721-3 pbk.

10 9 8 7 6 5 4 3 2 1
Manufactured in the United States of America

CONTENTS

FOREWORD

During the summer of 1976, Chet Fish, an old friend and an editor at the New York offices of David McKay, asked me to read a shotgunning book from England. It was this book, *Shooting—Why We Miss*, by Macdonald Hastings.

"We're thinking of publishing it in the United States," said Chet. "Do you think there's enough solid information here to interest the American sportsman?"

First I thumbed through the book and noticed drawings of shooters wearing knickers and funny hats. I could feel doubts begin to grip me. But I agreed to take the little book home and read it.

In chapter after chapter, Hastings confidently stated that a shooter should forget about lead (something he called forward allowance), aim with his arms, hit the trigger the instant the butt touched his shoulder, never look at the barrels, and so on. It all seemed like dreadful advice, especially for someone like me. I've been shooting behind birds for more than 20 years. Maybe some shooters can forget about lead, but not me. I have enough trouble knocking down grouse and woodcock.

But was Hastings on to something? Perhaps this unusual shooting style would work in the field. Since I'm always trying to figure out how not to miss a bird, I became interested. Hastings had convinced me that I should at least consider his technique, which seemed more natural and instinctive than some of the regimented shooting styles I had seen in the field and on clay-bird ranges.

Some time later, I was part of a group of *Outdoor Life* editors at the Campfire Club in New York, where we planned to burn up a lot of shells at trap and skeet. The shooting style of Macdonald Hastings had slipped from my mind until I saw John Fry, *Outdoor Life's* editorial director, take his turn at Station 1. John squeezed the butt of his shotgun under his arm and up into his armpit. I had never seen John handle a gun before, but if he fired a shotgun in that position, I thought to myself, he would surely break his nose. Then he called "Pull" and hit the trigger the instant the butt hit his shoulder.

Matt Birmingham, Chairman of the Board of Times Mirror Magazines, was next on the roster. When Matt took the same under-the-arm stance that John used, I started to think again about Hastings and his unusual style.

At the end of the day, over a jug of chilled Chablis, I learned from John and Matt that they had just returned from the Orvis Shooting School in Vermont, where they were taught this very same English shooting technique. Matt, a veteran bird hunter, seemed convinced that this shooting style would solve many problems once it was mastered, but he was having some difficulty "unlearning" some of the old shooting habits he had formed over the years.

When Chet finally asked me to edit this book for publication in the United States, I agreed. By then I was eager to cooperate with Macdonald Hastings, who was advocating a technique that was already affecting the shooting styles of some Americans, including myself. And we decided we'd have new drawings.

Besides, how can anyone ignore an Englishman who states, very confidently, that if we follow his steps every time, and do it right, "WE WOULD NEVER MISS."

Vin T. Sparano

May 1977

PREFACE

In this book I have incorporated relevant passages from an earlier work of mine which is now out of print. *How to Shoot Straight* (1967) was addressed to the novice. *Shooting—Why We Miss* is for experienced shots, as well as novices, whose form is not as good as it might be, or perhaps as good as it used to be. Its purpose is to reduce the number of misses.

M.H.
Feast of St. Hubert (1975)

SHOOTING— WHY WE MISS

Figure 1. PARTS OF A TYPICAL DOUBLE-BARREL SHOTGUN
Barrels:
1. FRONT SIGHT
2. RIB
3. EXTRACTORS
4. REAR LUMP
5. FORWARD LUMP
6. HOOK
7. FORE-END LOOP
8. FLATS SHOWING PROOF MARKS
9. CHAMBERS

Stock and action:
10. COCKING LEVERS
11. COMB
12. ACTION FACE
13. STRIKER HOLES
14. TOP LEVER
15. TOP STRAP OR TANG
16. SAFETY
17. TRIGGERS
18. TRIGGER GUARD
19. CHECKERING
20. HEEL
21. TOE

Fore-end:
22. CHECKERING
23. FORE-END
24. FORE-END TIP
25. RELEASE BUTTON

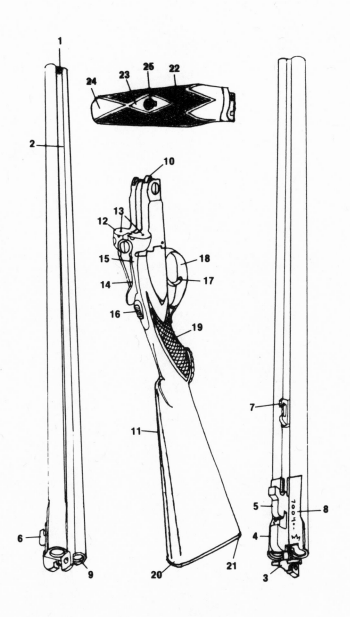

1
QUESTION
MARKS

You are not shooting as well as you did? You have never shot as well as you feel you ought to? Or as well as that rare shot, that very rare shot, who never seems to miss?

Perhaps you have not been as successful with your new gun as you were, or think you were, with the old gun which was your first gun?

If you are a young shot, you may be wondering whether you will ever make a good shot? If you are an old shot, you may suspect that you are getting past it; that it is time you packed it in?

Are you bruising your trigger finger, or your shoulder, on recoil? When you fire is the butt of your gun, as shotguns do when they don't like the way you handle them, kicking you in the jaw?

However much you try, does the game you shoot at seem to have tin drawers?

The aim of this book is to answer the questions you ask yourself on an off-day, to point out what might have gone wrong. More important it is designed to correct your mistakes, to show you how to make your own shooting much better.

I cannot teach you, I cannot teach myself, not to miss. The shooter, if he ever existed, who never missed would give up the sport out of sheer boredom. What is useless, if you wish to have the reputation of being a workmanlike shot, is to try to muddle through. Throughout this book, I have inserted axioms which might well be displayed in any gunroom. The first is the most important:

It does not matter if you miss. You have no excuse if you don't know why you missed.

The phrase "hit and miss" properly describes the wrong approach to any skilled sport. It is true that there are exceptional people, without any conscious style, who can do almost anything with some success. In shooting I have known gamekeepers who wielded their guns like hammers, and somehow got results, but they were not shooting for sport or, least of all, seeking the sporting shots which is a very important part of hunting. Most of us must play by the rules.

I can recall a story about a great coach showing a schoolboy how to use his bat. "Mickey Mantle," he said, "can take a swing at a bad pitch and get a hit. He's better than we are. You and I must play by the rules and take only the good pitches."

In shooting, as in baseball, and, as I shall show you later, in the techniques of playing golf, the game is the same. You must first conquer your own temperament. You must discipline yourself into learning a classic style. You must watch your swing, and never fail to take your eye off the ball.

I have patterned this book to help others who are as liable to miss as I am. I am just hopeful that I can give you some thoughts on why we miss.

2
FIRST AIM

If your forefinger was a shotgun barrel and your own arm a wooden stock you would inevitably find your mark every time you aimed at a moving target. When we point with a finger we do everything right. As soon as we sight an object the message goes into the arm. Starting slow from the waist, growing increasingly quicker, the movement of the arm is an impeccable gunmounting action.

True, you will miss if you subsequently try to hold your finger on the target. But the instant that you point is always the true one. The first look is accurate because the combination of eyes and hand could not have come about unless they were perfectly co-related. As Kipling would have written: *This is the law*. The problem is to apply it to the artificial limb, which your gun forms.

If you have had a bad day (and who hasn't?) you might well do worse than walk out without a gun under your arm and swing your finger at any passing target. Notice how sweetly your arm swings into action. Notice how your arm obeys your eye. That, at its briefest, is the secret of straight shooting.

4

Where we go wrong with a gun is when we think too much. We try and improve on our natural first aim. Indeed we try too hard. The result, almost invariably, is that we miss behind. I can kick myself now that I missed the easiest chance I ever had in my life of a right-and-left at woodcock—and, incidentally, winning a prize of a bottle of Wild Turkey bourbon—because I was so anxious to make sure of them that I missed both birds by a mile. My neighbor made two snap shots and killed both of them behind him. He hadn't the time that I had to think. Like Shakespeare's Cassius, it is dangerous for a shooter to think too much.

Indeed, once you start thinking too much, you will assuredly miss most of the birds you shoot at. You will poke rather than swing. You will go home remembering so seldom the times you did it all right, and so often the occasions when you did it all wrong.

A good example is how often, when a bird shows briefly in a gap between the branches of woodland trees, you can make what you believe is a wild shot, and drop it dead at your feet. Your friends will congratulate you on your marksmanship. In fact the sheer lack of time to think made sure that you fired on first aim. By contrast notice what a poor show even good guns will make when birds are flushed out of a field of roots and you can watch them coming for several hundred yards. The longer the wait, until they fly into range, the more anxious the shooters become. And anxiety is one of the worst enemies of good shooting. Second aim, which means a miss, is the usual concomitant.

A fine shot taught me how to deal with those birds you can see coming, it seems for minutes, over flat country. He bet me that he could kill a pheasant between the two of us before I could. He was a superb judge of distance and he beat me again and again by 15 yards or so. Further, he wouldn't look at the birds until he could hear them coming; or somebody called his name in warning. More significantly, he made snapshots of all of them. I lacked his confidence.

Confidence counts for so much. You will notice that if you kill the first head of game of the day, you will probably go on putting up a good performance. If you miss it you are likely to get worse and worse until the time when you feel you couldn't hit a crawling bus. It even happens to the best shots. Robert Churchill, the great gunmaker who was my mentor in shooting practice, used to say that if he was having an off day he conserved his cartridges. He fired one barrel instead of two, and patiently worked himself into form again. I protested to him that he was accustomed to shooting in Europe, where hundreds of head of driven game are offered to the gun on a single hunt. Most of us are lucky to have half-a-dozen chances in a day. But I know what he was getting at. He refused to be panicked.

If you are doing badly remember this paradox:

If you see your gun barrels, or hear your gun go off as you fire, you will miss.

The reason is that your mind is not concentrated on the target. If it was you wouldn't be looking at the barrels of your gun. If it was you would only subconsciously hear the explosion of the cartridge. If you draw a bead, if you are thinking of recoil, you are almost bound to shoot behind a moving target.

Novices consistently fall into the trap. Even experienced shots have their lapses and always will. The purpose of this book is to reduce the margin of misjudgment when you are handling what is definitively an extension of your own body. The chief way to success with a gun is to regard it as a part of yourself. These days, it is scarcely ever the cartridge's or the gun's fault if you miss. The problem is you and me.

You may accuse me in the succeeding pages of repeating myself. I make no excuse. This is a drill book, and the secret of drill is repetition. I have ordered it so that to begin with you get to know yourself. Later, I will propose how you can train, suggesting how to put things right when they seem to be going all wrong.

I have written throughout partly in the form of questions and answers in the hope that you will refer to this after cleaning your gun and ruefully counting an expensive waste of ammunition.

3
YOURSELF

In other books on shooting I have put "drill" first. But I am increasingly of the opinion that the conquest of temperament is even more important in the field than the knowledge of the correct way to handle a gun. People who are experts at breaking clay pigeons, with a predictable course and speed, are so often at fault when they are faced with a covey of quail, a curving pheasant, or a zigzagging hare. An animal or bird doesn't do what you expect it to do. The sheer excitement of an exploding covey of partridges is often enough to force an experienced gun to make all the mistakes in the book.

I remember an occasion when shotgun expert Robert Churchill was my guest on a bird hunt. A beautiful covey of partridges offered over his head. Just because he knew that all of us were expecting him to give us a lesson he never touched a feather. At multiple clay pigeons in his own shooting school he would have broken the lot. Because we were all looking at him as the maestro, he lost his nerve. He missed because the rest of us believed, and he was conscious that we believed it, that he couldn't miss. It floored him. He made up for it later; but it emphasizes my point that even if you know it all, you will miss if too much is expected of you, and you are thinking that too much is expected of you.

I was shooting on another occasion with A. G. Street, who had a great reputation as a top shotgun shot. He wouldn't have normally worried about missing, but we were standing in a line of guns, all within sight of each other and all with a critical eye on Street. The first bird that showed was a cock pheasant that flew straight over Arthur. With all eyes fixed on him, he killed it with a beautifully timed shot. Arthur told me afterward that he had never feared missing more in his life. He knew that the local hunters, mildly resentful of a man from another area, wanted him to miss. He needed to prove them wrong. His was a triumph not of straight shooting but of sheer personality. He wasn't going to let them panic him.

Yet it is a fact that most of us don't shoot as well as we can because we worry too much about what our personal performance is likely to be. In later chapters I intend to show how you can reduce failure by a discipline of gunmanship. But in the meantime it may be valuable to analyze what are possibly your personal anxieties in the field. They are important in shaping you into a good shot.

DO YOU PLAY GOLF?

That seems an odd question to start a book on straight shooting. It happens that the art of golf is the art of shooting. May I encourage you by adding that it is much easier to be a good shot than a top golfer. You have a far longer margin for error. But the game is the same.

The difference is that while nobody expects to play golf well without constant practice and study of the game, most men after an occasional day with a gun are disappointed with themselves if they fail to put up a good performance. The secret of straight shooting, like playing golf, is constant practice, a steady temperament, and a knowledge of the game.

Balance and swing are as important in shooting as in golf. As in golf the first lesson (and the last) is to keep your eye on the ball. If your eye wanders from your target in the middle of your swing you will assuredly miss. Curiously enough it doesn't matter which part of your target you fix your eyes on. Preferably the head. But a wingtip or a leg will do just as well. The spread of shot from your shotshell will cover the whole bird.

Later, I will explain to you how you must pick the ground for your feet as carefully, or almost as carefully, as a golfer does. You must learn to judge distance. Most of us are familiar with the 100 yards of a football field. The average oak or elm, which looks tall enough, is seldom taller than 50 to 60 feet; that is 20 yards or so. The effective range of a shotgun is somewhere between 30 and 50 yards. It may surprise you, but it's true, that most game is shot at a distance of about 18 yards. A kill at 30 yards is exceptional.

The average third floor windowsill is a mere 24 to 30 feet above ground level. So much for the birds that come higher than the trees.

That is why I asked, do you play golf? A golfer realizes how important it is to practice his eye at gauging distances. If you are standing 40 yards away from a belt of trees, for example, and the trees are 10 yards high, the extreme distance when a bird tops the trees will be about 45 yards and you will be more likely to overestimate the range than otherwise.

Golfers worry about the yards and the feet, and the inches. The shooting man needs to be not quite so careful but careful enough.

In the search for concentration, think first about distance, and the art of keeping your eye on the ball, which is your target.

DO YOU FEEL THAT YOU ARE BETTER WITH A RIFLE THAN A SHOTGUN?

Scarcely anybody is a first-class shot with a rifle and a shotgun at the same time. The reason is simply that a rifle is essentially a weapon of immobility, and a shotgun is a weapon of movement. If you are used to a rifle you will properly hang on the sights, estimating your range, allowing for windage, holding your breath for a steady shot. The method is hopeless if you are using a shotgun. In shotgun work it is essential that you follow your arm in the swing on to the target. If you pause to find a bead you will miss.

It is true that all shotguns have a bead on the end of their barrels. I am not quite sure what it is doing there except as an aid in a sitting shot. It is something the shotgun shooter should never see when he is swinging his gun. Admittedly it is true that there are some born shots—I think of some professional hunters in Africa I have known—whom I have seen bringing down running game with a rifle. It is a rare gift to be able to swing a single bullet into a moving target. I doubt if the men I have seen do it ever looked at their sights.

The fact is that all of us, when we are on our day, might kill with a single bullet. When you have the confidence you can kill in the center of a shotgun pattern every time. Churchill designed a .22 rifle for wildfowling. I was surprised how often I killed with it.

Confidence . . . Confidence . . . Confidence. That's what it's all about. So often, we all lack it.

ARE YOU NERVOUS IN STRANGE COMPANY?

This is a common complaint. You are invited to shoot in

unfamiliar company. You are supposed to know all about it, and you doubt if you do. You see the next man pull off a right-and-left, and you yourself miss abominably on a shot which you would never have missed if you were alone. I will give you the answer in the next question.

ARE YOU EATING AND DRINKING TOO MUCH, OR TOO LITTLE?

It is proper to say that a serious shot should obey Samuel Smiles' unctious injunction to bed early, rise early and practice a rigid abstemiousness. I cannot pretend that it works.

Cold sober is the worst mood for shotgun work. I have stayed up all night on a bird hunt playing poker, and shot better the next day than I did on the first. The reason was simply that I didn't give a damn whether I hit or I missed.

All that the illustration proves, in an amoral way, is the importance of forgetting to worry about why you hit or miss. If you stop worrying, and you know the important drill, which I shall explain in the next chapter, you will be surprised how good you can be.

ARE YOU WEARING THE RIGHT CLOTHES?

The clothes in which you look best are not necessarily the clothes in which you will shoot best. I treasure a copy of the Badminton Library book on shooting (1896) which divides the Good Sort from the Wrong Sort. The Wrong Sort wear fashionable shooting clothes, but they carry their guns in all the wrong dangerous ways. The right shots, in plain and durable field clothes, look as safe as houses. But I doubt if any one of those shooters wore the right clothes.

It is possible that, even at the present time, none of us have worked out the right clothes for a day's shooting. Everybody seems to have their own notion about it, which is normally eccentric.

Some English shotgunners had an idea that the best jacket for shooting was what is called a Raglan coat, named after that inefficient commander of British troops in the Crimean War. The style is cut with loose sleeves under the armpits. The trouble is that shooting is often done in a cold climate. The problem of keeping warm calls for heavy coats and sweaters. Waterfowl hunters are especially liable, and with good reason, to overclothe themselves.

Organize yourself to give the greatest ease of movement in your torso. Wear whatever you choose on your head, ear-flaps and all. You can wear two pairs of pants and two pairs of socks to keep warm, but don't smother your style by buckling up your shoulder blades.

DO YOU WEAR EYEGLASSES?

In most sports and games eyeglasses are a disadvantage. The disadvantage in shooting is negligible except on those occasions when the lens are blurred by rain. On those days you might well do worse than put your glasses into your pocket.

If you can recognize without the benefit of your glasses the difference between a grouse and a pheasant you are more likely to shoot straight than a "Dead-eye Dick" hanging on his aim. You are more likely to shoot on first aim. I remember one shotgun instructor telling me how he coached a half-blind man by sounding the whistle, and indicating to him in his blurred vision where the game was coming from. He killed remarkably. Before that he believed that he couldn't.

Few of us, in shotgun practice, can excuse ourselves on the grounds of poor eyes. What goes wrong is bad mounting, poor footwork, and sloppy head movement. I will deal with those problems in the next chapter.

Meanwhile, if you have been missing because you believe that your sight is not what it ought to be, you may assume that if you can pick up the number on a crosstown bus, you ought to be able to pull down any bird that flies over your head, or behind it.

DO YOU SHOOT WITH YOUR EYES OPEN?

The vast majority of shotgun work is best done with *both eyes open*. There are a few shots who seem to do better when they close one eye as if they were sighting a rifle. Nevertheless, it is an unusual practice tempting the shooter to look down his barrels instead of gluing his eye on the target. It also creates a tendency to make the fatal error, which I shall discuss later, of trying to "lead" a moving target so that your shot charge intercepts it.

ARE YOU EVER CAUGHT OFF BALANCE?

It is a common fault. A 12-gauge shotgun can be an unfriendly animal, just as it goes with you when you enjoy taking recoil into your legs. If you study the drill you can beat it. Recoil, which hurts novices, is easily beaten if you practice what I tell you. Even experienced shots, who do not watch their drill, can be thrown by a sudden shot when they are caught off balance. It sometimes means that the trigger finger is wrapped too closely around the guard. The kick of the gun bruises the finger. In practice you should only touch the trigger with the index tip. The rest of your hand should be well back on the small of the stock.

It is important that you study the rules of dry practice in the next chapter on style. You are less likely to make the mistakes that we are all prone to.

ARE YOU BETTER AT SOME GAMES THAN OTHERS?

Men who are good at shooting game flying away from them are sometimes hopeless at birds flying toward them when the whole atmosphere is different. I have seen men, reliable game shots under most conditions, completely lose their nerve when they are faced with a bursting covey of birds flying toward them. If you wish to be a workmanlike shot you must drill yourself—I am about to emphasize the drill—into an automatic reaction. I shall explain to you later how you ought to react to different species of game.

If you are missing, it is more important than ever to examine your style, and study all the tricks in shooting technique.

ARE YOU TRUSTING LUCK?

If that is what you are trusting to, you haven't a hope in hell of becoming a good shot. It is true that more people than in any other sport think that if they have a gun in their hands they can't go wrong. They are a murderous menace to everybody about them. They are unlikely to shoot anything they clumsily aim to hit. They are likely to injure or kill anybody foolish enough to go out into the field with them.

I remember an occasion when I went on a duck hunt in New York. During first light I realized that my fellow shooters all had centerfire rifles, as well as their pump shotguns, to intercept any passing deer. When a swamp deer approached they began to shoot all around me. I threw myself flat on my stomach and did not get up until the deer made a safe escape.

There is no luck in shooting. It is only discipline which counts. There is no luck in accurate shooting. It is only discipline which counts.

When we miss, we must recognize that it is due to lack of discipline.

DO YOU EVER SHOOT AT CLAYS?

You can learn shooting from a book. It takes longer than learning it from a shooting school. You can learn from me something that you will learn much quicker, at greater expense, from an expert who will introduce you to clay pigeon shooting.

Clay-bird shooting, such as trap and skeet, has its dangers. The reason is simply that the clay from a trap has a certain flight and trajectory. Clays can be difficult to hit, but you know approximately where they are going. The difference between clays and live game is that game comes unexpected. Birds do not always do what we expect them to do.

A good clay pigeon shot can be utterly unnerved when he meets live game in the field.

Nevertheless, there is no more important way of learning the rhythm of shooting than in a good clay-pigeon school. All I am going to say to you later about the importance of the position of hands, feet and head and the art of gunmounting which joins them all, you can learn quicker under a good coach.

DO YOU EVER DRILL YOURSELF IN BLANK PRACTICE?

If you are doing badly you had better follow me carefully in the next chapters. If you are thinking of giving it all up you will do well to get out your gun, and think again.

There is no better way of getting yourself back into form than going back to the basics.

4
THE THEORY OF
AUTOMATIC LEAD

It used to be the custom to teach sportsmen to draw a bead with the shotgun. The theory was that you calculated varying lead according to the speed and angle of the target. It was an appallingly complicated way of teaching shotgun work. It meant that the shooter had to make a rapid calculation of the speed and distance of the target, with allowance for the time lag in trigger-pulling and the action of the lock mechanism on the primer of the shotshell. Assuming the estimated speed of his quarry was 30 mph, he was supposed to allow 2.5 feet at 20 yards, 4 feet at 30 yards, 6 feet at 40 yards. The odds on the shooter getting the speed of the target right, the distance right, and timing his own reactions, were about as long as hitting the Daily Double at Hialeah on 10 consecutive days. Although shooting was taught like that, people who performed well with the shotgun, forgot lead. Otherwise they couldn't have shot as well as they did.

But, significantly, none of them gave a rational explanation as to how they achieved the results they did. It fell to the twentieth century gunmaker Robert Churchill to

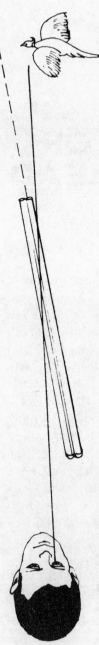

Figure 2. THE THEORY OF AUTOMATIC LEAD: The shooter's eyes are fixed on the bird. It is of no consequence whether the target is anything from a cock pheasant to a clay pigeon, whether it is moving fast or slow. If your eyes do not wander, they will automatically regulate the speed of your gun lift. If you hold your head steady, mounting slow, finishing quick, and touching the trigger the instant the butt hits your shoulder, you can forget all calculations. You don't *aim* with a shotgun at a flying object. You should use your shotgun like your own arms, as an extension of your own body. If we could all do this right, every time, we would never miss.

pioneer a new method of teaching people to shoot straight. It is the method I am advocating here.

Dismissing the traditional theory that the way to shoot at a moving target is to place your gun to intercept it in the air, Churchill taught that the first principle is the first principle of any ball game. Keep your eye on the target. If your eye wanders to the extent that you see your gun barrel, worst of all the bead on the end, or your attention lapses just enough so that you think about recoil, you will miss.

Figure 2 shows how the theory works in actual practice. The shooter's eyes are fixed on the bird but the angle of the barrels of the gun is in front of the target. When bird and barrel come into view together, if there is no hesitation, if the head is held correctly, the necessary lead is automatically provided.

Just knowing that is only a beginning to the art of straight shooting. You will miss if you try too hard; hang on to the trigger; or make a fault of style with hands, feet, or head. You will never be a consistent shot, until, having mastered the drill, you have acquired *muscle memory*.

When you go for a walk or a swim, you don't have to think to yourself how you do it. As a baby you had to learn to walk. Most of us can remember how we floundered about when we were learning to swim. You have to learn how to shoot. Once learned you don't have to think how you do it anymore. Muscle memory asserts itself.

When you miss, you will know why you missed. With practice, you will even learn where you miss. You will settle down perhaps not as a great shot but as a consistent one. In time, you will develop your own style.

For the present, follow the instructions in the drill section, in the next chapter, as though you were on the parade ground and I am the sergeant-major. The difference is that, unlike the sergeant-major, I have endeavored to explain, again and again, why you should do what I tell you.

Ideally, you should study the drill with this book on the table and the gun—an empty one!—at your side for dry practice. At this stage, you are not to pull the trigger. Indeed, you should never pull the triggers of an empty gun. The release of the triggers jars the action. If you must pull the triggers, load the chambers with empty shotshells or snapcaps which you can get at any gun shop.

5

AFTER THE THEORY, THE PRACTICE

This is the "barracks" chapter, in which you must discipline yourself like a soldier. Unlike a soldier, you have to do it, unless you go to an expensive shooting school, on your own. If you can afford it, I recommend anybody to sharpen up on clay pigeons under the guidance of an expert who will tell you what you are doing wrong.

While I can only suggest ways of conquering your personal temperament, I can tell you unequivocally how to manage your gun. I am assuming that you are a reasonably experienced shot; that you know how to clean your weapon; and that you know how to use it with safety in the presence of other people, not excepting when you are on your own. My purpose in this chapter is to explain the elements of using a shotgun. You can practice the drill without firing a shot. Just go through the movements.

Throughout I am addressing myself to right-shouldered shots. If you are a left-hander you will need to reverse the instructions.

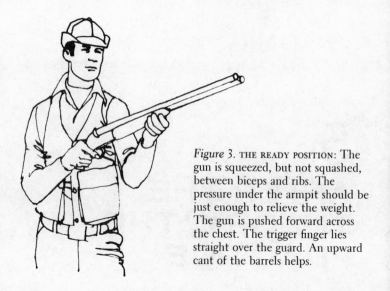

Figure 3. THE READY POSITION: The gun is squeezed, but not squashed, between biceps and ribs. The pressure under the armpit should be just enough to relieve the weight. The gun is pushed forward across the chest. The trigger finger lies straight over the guard. An upward cant of the barrels helps.

It may seem absurd to you that the way you hold your gun before shooting starts is important. In fact, it is half the battle.

In readiness for gun-mounting, the stock must be tucked well in underneath the arm. You are inviting a miss if you hold the gun loosely with the butt at elbow level. Place the stock with the small of the butt just forward of the right armpit, and squeeze it between biceps and ribs. Do not squeeze it so tightly that you are constricting yourself. The important thing is to feel firm, confident and collected. Don't make yourself so taut that you sacrifice smoothness of action.

In any other position, there is an inclination to rush the gun to the shoulder with the result that it never comes to the same place twice running. To do that is to invite a miss. Consistency in style is a vital concomitant to consistent shooting. The method advocated here, practiced until it becomes automatic, will compel you to do the right thing.

Tuck the stock well under your arm: (1) You must *push*

your left hand forward as you mount not merely raise it;
(2) I want you to push your left hand forward because your
left hand is your aiming hand; (3) By thrusting your left
hand into the aim the recoil of the charge will travel
through your left arm and thence through your frame; (4)
By squeezing the gun under your armpit, you are taking
weight off your hands and encouraging the muscles in your
arms to relax.

There are other advantages in making the ready position
a firm habit. It is the quickest form of gun-mounting
because the butt simply has to slip a few inches from
underarm to shoulder without losing contact with your
body. The gun comes smoothly and naturally to eye level;
(5) The gun comes up to your face instead of the head
going down to meet the stock. Faulty head movement is
one of the most common causes of poor shooting; (6) The
system checks hasty gun-mounting and encourages correct
timing; (7) It prevents the incidence of a bruised cheek
and jawbone from the recoil; (8) It encourages the right

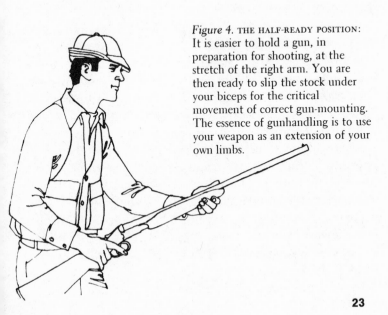

Figure 4. THE HALF-READY POSITION:
It is easier to hold a gun, in
preparation for shooting, at the
stretch of the right arm. You are
then ready to slip the stock under
your biceps for the critical
movement of correct gun-mounting.
The essence of gunhandling is to use
your weapon as an extension of your
own limbs.

hand to adopt the correct position inside the stock and prevents a bruised middle finger; (9) It keeps you squarely onto your target because your body is checked from turning too much sideways, but it also encourages you to adopt a natural stance.

Finally, and this is most important of all, it helps you to start your body swing while the gun is coming up.

Let's go back to the beginning again. Sway the gun on your wrist with your right hand only. Then, one-handed, lift the butt to your shoulder. The gun will feel top heavy. *Your right hand is your gun-raising hand.* Now lay your left hand on the fore-end of the gun with your extended thumb pointing straight up the barrels in a line parallel with the extended index finger. *Your left hand is your aiming hand.*

With both hands in position, tuck the butt of the gun under your arm. It is no use holding the gun slackly with the butt at elbow level. You must place the stock well under your armpit. You must feel the wood with a squeeze. Generally speaking it is a good notion to slant the barrels slightly skyward.

When you go into the "ready" position, your right hand should be round the small of the stock, index finger extended to cover the guard, left hand round the fore-end, thumb extended, the butt of the gun underneath your arm. In that position use your left arm to push the barrels of the gun across your chest, so that they are pointing not to the left but straight in front of you.

At first, this will seem an unnatural position. In fact, the position is the first step toward the achievement of consistent shooting. The stock is well tucked under your arm so that when you mount the gun to your shoulder, you will give a forward push, and not a lift. A mere lift means that the barrels of your gun are swinging all over the place. A push forward means that your left hand, the aiming hand, is doing its proper job.

By thrusting your left hand into the aim, the recoil of

the charge travels through your left arm, down through your frame, which will take it like soft rubber. Otherwise you catch it on the shoulder where you will find it hurts.

By squeezing the gun under your armpit—squeezing in the love sense—you are taking weight off your hands and helping the muscles of your arms to relax.

Most important of all, the "ready" position is a preparation for correct gun-mounting. It is a position designed to train you to thrust your shoulder into the stock when you fire. It will help you to avoid a common error—the error which results in more misses than most—of dragging your stock into your shoulder.

You must thrust your shoulder into the butt of the gun. The gun should never be mounted against a flinching shoulder.

There are other advantages in making the "ready" position a firm habit. It is the quickest form of gun-mounting because the butt simply has to slip a few inches from under arm to shoulder without losing contact (this is important) with your body. The gun comes smoothly, naturally, without a snatch to eye level. The gun comes up to your face instead of your head coming down to meet the stock. Faulty head movement, as I shall explain, is one of the commonest causes of faulty shooting. The system checks hasty gun-mounting and encourages good timing. It will force you to start your body swing as the gun is coming to your shoulder. To adopt it comfortably, you will find yourself standing the way you ought to be, square on target.

WHERE ARE YOU PUTTING YOUR FEET?

Remember the trouble good golfers take to find a balanced and comfortable stance. Good guns are equally particular. You will notice that, when game flies over rough ground, experienced shots take care to secure a position for their feet in which they can pivot without obstruction. They stamp the ground in the same way a baseball player does home plate.

Figure 5A. WRONG: Feet placed too wide. The gun will punish you for standing like this. You have no freedom of movement.

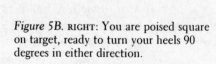

Figure 5B. RIGHT: You are poised square on target, ready to turn your heels 90 degrees in either direction.

I appreciate that, on some hunts, you may be in a blind and not on your feet at all. First, the drill is how to shoot standing up on your two feet. The rest will follow.

With your gun at the "ready" position, look down at your legs. In the correct shooting attitude your body should be balanced evenly between them. If you are of medium height, the toes of your feet should be about nine inches apart, and the heels about three inches. A taller man, may extend his feet for comfort a little more. But it is better to take too narrow a stance than one which is too wide. If you put a gun into the hands of a novice—an ideal

Figure 6A. WRONG: Your stance is too narrow. You will be off-balance, and catch recoil when you fire.

Figure 6B. WRONG: The "aggressive" stance with left foot too far forward, usually accompanied by a flinching shoulder.

subject for the experiment is an average girl—you will notice that when she mounts it, she instinctively draws back her right shoulder from the butt and advances her left foot. What is meant to be an aggressive stance is just the opposite.

Don't place your feet too wide, otherwise you will be off balance when you fire. The recoil of the charge will lift the butt from your shoulder to your arm muscles. You will

Figure 7A. SWINGING TO RIGHT BEHIND: Scrape right foot behind left. Pivot on left toe.

Figure 7B. SWINGING TO LEFT BEHIND: Scrape left foot behind right. Pivot on right toe.

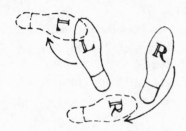

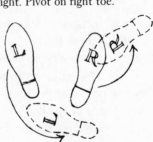

probably bruise yourself, and you will assuredly shoot underneath the target crossing on the right, and over the top of one moving to the left. You will be all over the place with the second barrel.

If you stand with your heels too close together, you will find that you are taking the recoil on your shoulder instead of down your legs where you won't feel it. If you come home from a day's shooting with a bruised cheek or a bruised second finger, don't blame the gun. The chances are that you have been shooting from a stance which is too narrow for you.

It's equally a fault to spread your legs too wide. Try it, and you will find that you are unable to transfer your body weight from one foot to another without swaying your trunk. Consequently, when you fire you will drop your shoulder and miss underneath. On rough ground, recoil can knock you off your feet.

The ideal position is exactly the same as a good golfer adopts to swing a club. The balance on both legs is even, your body is poised to drain gun recoil pleasurably through your boots. Without a gun in your hand, it is a position in which you can swing your shoulders rhythmically, with only a minimal change of weight from one leg to the other. When you are satisfied that you have found the position that suits you best, pick up your gun in the "ready" position. Without lifting your gun to your shoulder, practice the swing of 45 degrees to the right and to the left. The swing to the left will transfer the weight onto your left leg. The swing to the right will transfer it to your right leg.

Now increase the swing to 90 degrees in both directions. You will find that, as you pass 45 degrees, you will raise your heels and pivot on your toes with the movement. Ideally, your stance should not change in the half-circle to left or right. In practice, especially on rough ground, it is sometimes advisable to move one foot to the rear of the other. But the theory remains.

Only one leg moves. The other is the prop on which
your gun is mounted.

At this stage of dry practice, resist if you can the
inclination to mount the gun to your shoulder. Keep the
butt tucked underneath your arm. The reason that *more
than half the misses in shooting are made before gun-
mounting.* You must get footwork and body swing right
first.

It is so important that shooting coaches often demon-
strate how, with correct timing, you will shoot straight at a
moving target even if you press the trigger before your
shoulder has bedded into the butt of the gun. Some grouse
shots, though I don't recommend it, do just that in the
field.

A lot of your shooting may be from a walking position,
but don't get the impression that what I'm telling you
about footwork may be all very well with a comfortable
stand on a dove field but not for a man who has to march
out and find his game. If you want to shoot straight,
there's no difference.

However unexpected the shot, there is always time if
you cultivate muscle memory, to find your feet as you
shoot. Remember that, if you let off with your left foot
forward, you will shoot under the mark. If you shoot with
feet together, you will be off balance and catch recoil.
Your second barrel will simply be a waste of ammunition.

There's always time—not to take aim with a shotgun
because if you do that you will miss—but to collect
yourself into a balanced pose.

Up to now, I have counselled you, in dry practice, not to
mount the gun to your shoulder. The secret of any drill, as
any sergeant knows, is to learn it stage by stage and to
repeat until the recruit hardly has to think what he's
doing. I can only insist that, if you want to be a
consistently good shot, you can't afford to skip any stage.

In the "ready" position, let's make an experiment. Later on, I'll have more to say about gun-mounting. For the moment, concentrate on hands. Most people believe that they grip a gun naturally and correctly. Check your own grip. A common fault is to wrap the *right hand* too far over the top of the stock. Wrap your fingers as far round the small of the stock as they will go and you will find that you can't lift the gun without raising your elbow as well. If you shoot from that position, the recoil will bash the knuckle of your second finger against the rear of the trigger-guard. Another fault is for shooters with a short thumb to keep it in contact with the top lever.

The correct position of the right hand is the one in which the small of the stock is sunk comfortably in the palm of your hand. In that position, the ball of your trigger finger—the pad of your finger not the first joint— should be lying along the guard just within pressing distance of the trigger. You should see a clear gap of daylight between the back of the trigger finger and the knuckle of your second finger. When you fire, your right hand simply has the duty of lifting the stock from the "ready" position, the mere six inches it should travel, until it settles into the thrust of your shoulder. Your trigger finger should scarcely move because *triggers on shotguns should never be pulled*. All your trigger finger will apply is a slight stiffening in pressure to meet the thrust of your shoulder into the gun, the forward balanced movement of your whole body into the butt.

Forget "pulling" the trigger. If you have a good gun, a slight stiffening of pressure on the pad of your finger and your shoulder thrust forward to meet the butt is what is wanted. Remember that your *left hand* is your raising hand. Your left hand has the duty of raising your gun to your shoulder, but your left hand is also your *aiming hand*.

With the sole evidence that the muzzle must have been pointing correctly at the target, it is obviously misleading to think of shotgun work in terms of aiming with your barrels. That is unless your ambition rises no higher than a sitting target. All you have to make sure of is that the extended thumb of your left hand, lying along the barrel, is pointing in the right direction. Leave the gun to look after itself. *It will shoot wherever your left hand puts it.*

I can believe that at this stage you may find it difficult to accept the rule of good shots: "Don't point with shotgun barrels." The "natural" thing to do—how often the natural theory is wrong—is to put the gun to your shoulder, aim upward and pull. Shooting that way, it would be a fluke if you hit the hat of your worst enemy when he throws it in the air.

The system of straight shotgun shooting is that if the left hand is moving smoothly onto the mark, as the gun is mounting, the barrel will be on the mark, too. We will come back to that, again and again, later. The secret of drill is repetition. At this stage, pick up your gun, the small of the stock in your right hand, make sure it is comfortably cupped in your palm, and that your trigger finger is extended within pad-reach of the front trigger and that you can see daylight behind the guard.

Now go back to the "ready" position. You may well have it right, but how tight are you holding your gun? My guess is that by this time you are hanging on to it like a tug-of-war rope. Relax. In dry practice, get the habit of hugging the butt of your gun under your arm as affectionately as a pretty girl, but as gently as one you cherish. It is only as you lift the gun to meet your shoulder, that you put on the pressure, tightening *only* at the moment that you touch the trigger. If you try too much as you lift into action you will relax too far and miss. The movement in ballroom dancing terms is slow—quick—quick. Start gentle—finish hard.

ARE YOU WATCHING YOUR HEAD?

Head movement is the cause of one half of the misses in shotgun shooting. You can prove it for yourself. Point your finger at any object. If you close one eye you will find that you come onto it first aim every time. Now lower your head as you raise your finger. Just notice how wide you are of the mark.

For guidance, practice with a gun in front of a mirror. If you see your head coming down to meet the stock, practice until you are confident that you are not bending your neck to your gun. Shooting is a proud business in which a proud head is vital to success.

Your head should only move on your shoulders with a gun in your hand, with the movements of your whole body. Don't hang it to kiss the gun. Raise the gun to your shoulder at the level of your head.

After all that drill, the secret that I want to impress on you is that you must master yourself. All you really have to do is to concentrate, keep your eye on the target, count it dead before you press the trigger, trust your first aim (you will miss if you look for a second one), and cultivate what I can only call an attitude of bloody-mindedness.

Nobody ever shot straight who was overanxious. The bird that flies away is the one you have promised for dinner, or the one you wanted to show your buddy that you couldn't miss. Good shooting is seldom hasty, rarely overcautious. You must master the drill. Without it, you won't know why you missed a haystack, or hit it. But, with a sound knowledge of the elements of the game, you will always know *why* you miss.

The next chapter concerns probably the most critical process of shotgun shooting for it coordinates all the mechanical functions of stance, footwork, head position and grip with a conscious function of aim.

6
GUN-MOUNTING AND STYLE

The compound movement of gun-mounting calls for an effort as complex—wait for it—as driving a car. Most of us can be relaxed enough at the wheel to listen to a radio or talk to a passenger, sometimes both at once, in the serene confidence that in the unforgiving moment we will apply the correct controls. To be a stylish shot you need to acquire the same sort of instinctive memory. Otherwise you will be left, in test after test in the field, with your learner plates.

I left you in the last chapter in the ready position, the butt of the gun squeezed between biceps and rib cage, barrels canted slightly upward with your gaze raised a few inches over the muzzles into the sky. You are a soldier standing at a sort of attention. You are ready to lift your gun into your shoulder.

To begin, let's start at the climax of the lift because you won't get there if you don't know at the beginning where the butt of the gun needs to be seated in your shoulder.

The best way of finding the precise position is to fold

Figures 8A and 8B. BODY MOVEMENT AIMS THE GUN: The positions frozen in the diagrams are, in actual practice, part of a continuous stream of action. If the movement is unbalanced, or if there is the slightest hesitation in trigger-pressing as the shoulder thrusts into the butt of the gun, it will be a miss. The rule is still the same when you are squatting in a blind waiting for a duck. Only then you must swing your shoulders from the waist, thrusting your shoulder even more purposefully into the butt of your gun as you press the trigger. Practice swings from your torso while you are waiting for game to show will loosen you up.

your arms across your chest. You will notice that your shoulders round forward with the movement in just the manner that your right shoulder should come forward to meet the butt. With your left hand feel "the slot" which the folded arms position has created between your collar bone and the ball in your shoulder socket. That is exactly where the butt plate of the gun should settle when you mount. Feeling it, you can almost believe that the human body has been anatomically fitted to take it.

Pick up your gun in the ready position, squeezing the stock under the gentle pressure of your biceps, and pushing the barrels away from your chest so that they are pointing not across your body but in front of you.

Now give the gun a slightly forward thrust with your left hand just sufficient to enable you to slide the butt plate up your arm to "the slot" in your advancing shoulder (the cross-armed shoulder position). The movement of the gun should be limited to the bare minimum to travel it from point to point. Ideally, the butt should never lose touch with the cloth of your jacket. The slightest clearance

Figures 9A and 9B. THE INSTANT OF TRIGGER-PRESSING: For a bird on the right (Figure 8A), the body is propped on the right leg. The left heel lifts and the left toe swivels in coordination with the movement of arms and shoulders onto the line of the target. For a bird on the left (Figure 8B), the weight is placed firmly on the left leg. Shooting at ground game coming from the left (Figure 9A), the weight is on the left leg and the shoulders lean forward to decline the body angle. At ground game coming from the right (Figure 9B), the body sways forward onto the right leg. The pivot of the toe and the twist of the heel away from the target enable the shooter to cover a field of 90 degrees on each side and to return, on the completion of the movement, to ready position.

between butt plate and shoulder is all that is necessary, or desirable. The thrust of the left arm automatically provides it.

Look out that you don't make a meal of the job, see-sawing the butt and barrels. The action must be as economical in traverse as you can make it, the gun rising in even balance to the level of your eyeline. Remember that it is fatal to drop your head to meet the lifting gun.

Practice with a stiff neck until you find the gun slipping smoothly into "the slot" in your shoulder and into the line of your vision.

This is the first lesson, but only the first lesson in gun-mounting. It is simply an exercise in preparation for the critical business of trigger-pulling. In actual shooting practice, the butt of the gun will not meet the thrust of your shoulder except at the instant you fire.

So easy to tell, so evasive in the conditions of the field. But practice . . . practice . . . practice . . . will help you command the situation.

Your instinct, especially when you are shooting badly, will mislead you again and again into putting the butt of your gun into your shoulder, taking a peep, and pulling later. You will be yards behind a moving target. You must discipline yourself to shoot on first aim. Second thoughts in game shooting are wasted ammunition.

The worst mistake you can make is to try and cut off a moving target by shooting at a space in front of it. Leading your bird is as hopeless a system of shooting as trying to pick up an object with your pointing finger when your eyes are looking in another direction. You will make a fluky kill once in a while. What you will never make is a consistent shot.

I have explained the theory of lead, because so few people seem to understand it, in a later chapter. But its interest, for practical shooting purposes, is eclectic. For the present, forget it. The knowledge of why you can shoot with a shotgun, without conscious aim, will not help you in the field to kill one bird more, or less.

Get the drill right, but remember that the drill is merely the exercise for field conditions. Even if you have learned to accomplish all the parade ground orders, your gun will be a lifeless log until you master AGGRESSION AND TIMING.

The top practitioners in all games recognize the importance of the will to win. It is tremendously important in the sport of shooting. If you are shy of your gun, a little lacking in confidence as to your capacity to use it, or to shoot hard and straight at what you are aiming at, you might just as well play checkers. The principle that if you grasp the nettle it won't sting is the principle of handling a shotgun.

A 12-gauge gun can sting. It can knock a tooth out, bruise a lip or cheek, or knock you on your butt if you recoil from it. But if you put your right shoulder into the work, cultivate a balanced action, and underline your determination with a swear word when you miss, you are more than half-way to the sound shot I want to make you. A sense of controlled aggressiveness is a vital attitude.

Timing means the smooth and balanced rate of lift of the gun from the ready position to the instant of firing. In practice, you will complete your gun-mounting quicker for a fast bird than a slow one. But ignore the reason why. Just trust your eye. Whether you hit or miss, providing the target is in range, will be decided during the brief lift of the gun from under your arm to your shoulder.

Waiting for a shot in the field, you should be holding your gun in the ready position firmly but without any sense of muscular strain. When you see the chance of a shot, glue your eyes on the target. Sway onto the correct foot and, at the same time, start a slow lift of the gun, increasing the pace as your eyes instruct you to follow. As your shoulder thrusts into the butt plate, harden your neck muscles, and stiffen your trigger finger—remember that it is a pressure not a pull—to fire.

I ought to add here that the word "pull" on the trigger is a bad one. It is a general term, and I plead as guilty as other people in the use of it. If your triggers need pulling, it is high time that your gun went back to the maker or a gunsmith for adjustment (see Chapter 10, *The Care of Guns*). You should never have the need to pull the triggers. A tightening of the pad of your index finger as you thrust your shoulder into the butt is the only proper way to shoot at moving targets.

The thrust of your shoulder into the gun should put the pressure on the pad of your trigger finger to fire.

Admittedly, it is easy to talk about it in theory. In practice, you must keep on reminding yourself that you must follow your eyes onto the target.

You mount your gun slow-slow-quicker-bang as you would your own arm.

Most of this instruction so far is for the oncoming or going-away bird in which very little body-movement is called for. If body-balance is composed, if the eye doesn't wander off the target, and if gun-mounting and trigger-pressing is well timed and aggressively controlled, these shots are the easiest to take. But most shooting calls for a swing to left or right, or behind. This is where footwork is vital. Besides correlating gun-mounting and eyes, your whole body must pivot with the gun.

The thrust of your shoulder into the butt must be timed to coincide exactly with the completion of the body swing.

Since most shotguns are doubles or repeaters, you may wonder why I haven't referred more to the second shot. To begin with, concentrate on the successful use of the first. It saves money.

Don't try and punch with two fists until you have made sure that you can deliver a knock-out with one. But, once you have mastered the rhythm of shotgun work, don't hesitate to use the second barrel; and use it quickly. It is especially useful on occasions when, after trying too hard with the first, you have missed behind. You will discover how often you can make a clean kill with a slightly exasperated snap shot with the second. It is proof of the importance of first aim. But make a rule never to fire the second shot, however quickly you do it, without dropping the gun from your shoulder, and mounting and swinging again.

There are born shots who can achieve balanced shooting with two shots from one mounting. They are very rare. Most people after recoil are off target. Simply start again. You will soon learn how quickly you can recover your poise; much quicker, in fact, than any bird flies.

If it was as easy to acquire in practice what I have explained in theory, this manual could end here. If it was easy, there could be no fun in shotgun shooting. Surprisingly, many of the born shots who hardly ever miss have difficulty in explaining how easily they hit. It is not much help for the rest of us puzzling to find out why we are so often off-target.

If you know why and where you miss, you are more than halfway toward becoming a good shot.

7
LEARNING WHY WE MISS

The value of DRILL and the importance of TIMING can be demonstrated in a way which, at first, seems like a conjuring trick. Watching another man's performance in the field, taking care not to look at what he is shooting at but his style, it is possible to assess with a high degree of accuracy whether he has made a hit or a miss. With experience, you will be able to achieve it yourself.

If you see a man windmilling his gun, dropping his head, pulling his shoulder away, fumbling with his feet, or hesitating for a poke at the target before snatching at the trigger, you may depend upon it that he has missed. But if you see the gun lifting calm-slow-quick-quicker in a rhythmic thrust with the whole body leaning on the movement, you don't have to look when you hear the bang to mark a clean kill.

If you see a shooter moving well on his legs, lifting his gun in an unhurried composed movement, firing in the instant that he throws his shoulder into the butt of his gun you will almost assuredly find, when you look up, that his bird is coming down. But if he is stiff-legged, hesitates when his gun comes up, do not be surprised to see his bird go over without losing a feather. The man who is on his day makes it *look* easy. The man whose gun-mounting *looks* hasty and clumsy, who rushes his second shot when he misses his first, makes it *look* difficult.

These days, when so many people have home movies, and everybody knows somebody who has a camera, it is valuable to get a friend to film action sequences of your own performance. You will be able to spot your own faults.

In ball games, everybody recognizes the true professional, the man with the controlled mastery of movement

Figure 10. MORE OR LESS RIGHT: Theoretically this is the safest way to carry a shotgun. The gun is laid across the shoulder, guard uppermost, with a protective forefinger on the trigger guard. The position is only dangerous if the barrels are permitted to trail. Not to be recommended, because other guns do not know whether you are loaded or not; or what will happen if you trip and fall, or drop your barrels behind.

Figure 11. RIGHT: In practice, the safest way to carry a gun is broken under your arm. The gun carries better. Your friends can see that the chambers are empty. You will gain points for care, far more than you will for a killing shot when others are unready. Make a rule that you will only get into the ready-loaded position when the hunt is on and you are in position to shoot.

in every nerve sinew. In the sport of shooting, too, you must make your stroke with unfaltering decision and follow through gracefully with your gun. In fact, a man who can shoot two birds out of a covey in front of him, then swing around and take a third behind, achieves a balance of timing and movement comparable to an athlete first-class. Very few can attain that sort of perfection in marksmanship.

But, when you do it right, to the onlooker it will seem easy. More than that, you yourself will feel on your day that it is. But not even the best are on their day all the time. I want to help you to shoot yourself back into form when everything seems to be going wrong.

On some days in the field, you will often find that you are shooting incorrectly because you are hurting yourself with recoil. If your shooting style was perfect—and nobody's is perfect all the time—you should theoretically stand up to five hundred rounds with no inconvenience except a healthy muscular fatigue. In practice, even the most hardened shots show a falling off in their performance after a hundred and fifty rounds or so.

The sense of occasion, in addition to the effort of concentration, also affects shooters. Some men, who shoot well when they are alone, find it difficult to get the best out of themselves among hunters they do not know well. They are tense and they try too hard. The excitement of unexpectedly good hunting also leads to errors in style, errors which will show in trifling discomforts. I have never heard of anybody who completely avoided them. But you should know the causes, and the way to set about overcoming them.

DO YOU SUFFER FROM BRUISED RIGHT FINGER?

It is one of the most common of shooting complaints. It is caused by the back of the trigger guard hitting the knuckle on recoil. This happens for one of three reasons: (1) You have held the gun too loosely at the instant of firing with the consequence that you have taken recoil on the middle knob of your finger; (2) You have failed, in gripping the small of the butt, to leave any space between your second finger knuckle and the back of the trigger-guard. You may well find that your forefinger has been hooked too far round the trigger; (3) You have raised your right elbow too high, thus slackening your grip when it must be firm.

Remind yourself, even if the stock of your gun is short for you, that you must hold back your right hand so that you only touch the trigger with the pad of your forefinger. If you can't do this with comfort, you would be well-advised to lengthen the stock of your gun with a pad over the butt.

ARE YOU EVER TROUBLED WITH BRUISED CHEEK OR JAW?

This is an affliction which commonly affects tall long-necked men like the writer. Short square men seldom suffer from it. It is a difficult fault to beat, especially in a hard day's shooting. Causes may be (1) that the stock is mounting a bit too wide of the correct gun-mounting position; (2) that the head is held too erect; (3) that the head is lowered at the moment of firing.

Theoretically, you should turn your head slightly away to avoid the trouble. Don't sandwich the flesh of your cheek like a piece of ham between jawbone and stock.

I myself have never altogether learned how to fire several hundred rounds without giving myself a slightly swollen jaw. I am content to be vulnerable. Providing you don't flinch, a sore jaw doesn't seriously affect shooting performance.

ARE YOU AFFLICTED WITH GUN HEADACHE?

This trouble befalls people who hold their heads too loosely. The old remedy of checking the vibration by biting a rubber band between the teeth is often effective. But better by far to learn to stiffen the neck muscles.

ARE YOU A VICTIM OF BRUISED MOUTH, BRUISED ARM, BRUISED SHOULDER, OR BRUISED CHEST?

Novices, firing shotguns for the first time, commonly split a lip or raise a bruise in full technicolor on the shoulder. It can be therapeutically useful to remind them what they have in their hands. The causes are loose grip, weak gun-mounting, flinching and fear of recoil. The cure is to learn the elements of the drill, or give up shooting.

It is wise to regard any symptom of discomfort from shooting as the consequence of an error in style. If you eliminate it without artificial aids, it must improve your performance.

Learn why you miss; never blame your cartridge. It is possible, although it is odds against it, that you may miss because of a hole in your shot pattern. But you can assume that the standard modern shotshell throws an unbelievably regular pattern which opens up, as it leaves a 12-gauge gun, to give you a cone of shot—because it has depth as well as width—about the diameter of a garbage can lid at the average distance at which most game birds, and clay pigeons, too, are killed. In brief, your shotshells provide you with a reliable and generous margin for minor errors of gun-mounting.

But if you are shooting with a borrowed gun, or a gun which doesn't fit you—for example, too long in the stock or too short in the stock for your own length of arm—you may be entitled to blame the gun. You cannot hope to shoot your best with an ill-fitting shotgun any more than you can look your best in ill-fitting clothes. I can only tell you that you can do something, if your arms are limber, to fit yourself to a weapon by modifying your grip. But it is no use pretending that you will shoot as well as you will with a gun which fits you.

You can also miss by wearing the wrong clothes. Waterfowlers, and I don't blame them, have a way of padding up to protect themselves against the wet and icy blast on their dawn hunts. But heavy clothes militate against clean, smooth shooting. Generally speaking, a waterfowler should use a gun shorter by a quarter to half-an-inch. For upland shooting, the best clothes are the same old clothes you have worn for years.

So far, after emphasizing the importance of drill, I have given reasons why you miss. I want to explain to you now

45

how you miss; and show you a method by which, however thin your pocket, you can teach yourself to correct mistakes.

You need two friends to help you. If a clay-pigeon trap is out of your class, toss an empty beer can. However you contrive it, the object is to show a moving target, any sort of target, against the sky. One friend is needed to spring the trap, the other to stand behind you as observer.

Your observer's job is to watch the shot in the air. Don't be surprised if, when you make the proposition, your buddy regards you as a raving lunatic. To shooting men who haven't tried, the notion that you can see a charge of shot in the air is as preposterous as believing in fairies. But, once the knack is acquired of knowing where to look and what to look for, it is within the capacity of anyone with reasonable eyesight. It is the trade secret of professional shooting coaches. They can see where you are shooting.

During the war, it was commonplace for people behind a howitzer to mark the trajectory of a shell lobbing through the air. The howitzer shell is a big object, but the initial velocity is not much higher than a shotgun charge. To play this game, you have to get rid of the factor of personal disbelief. The observer can do it, if he can persuade himself that he can.

Don't imagine that anybody can see a swarm of individual pellets. What an observer will see is a sort of aerial disturbance. In soft light conditions, it is even possible to mark it like an exploding balloon.

The man who is shooting cannot see it. The reason is that, although we describe our ammunition as smokeless, they throw both smoke and flame. If you are shooting on a still day, in a heavy stagnant atmosphere, you will see the smoke. If you are shooting at dusk, you will see the flame, spitting about two to three inches beyond the muzzle. The muzzle blast of flame, smoke and a disturbance of hot gases about as big as an orange, screens the vision of the man whose shoulder is thrust into the butt of the gun.

At this juncture, I can imagine a keen shooting man reflecting that it would surely be simpler to use tracer ammunition than set up the three-pronged operation I am recommending. Simpler, yes. The snag about tracers, although they look fine spouting out of the gun, is that, at the critical moment, the man who is using them loses sight of the line of the tracer behind the screen of muzzle blast and barrel lift which accompanies recoil. An onlooker may have seen the charge pass in front of the target. The man who is shooting, temporarily unsighted by muzzle blast, supposes that he has shot behind because the bird has gone on, and the tracer line has stayed up.

If tracers were the answer, they would be used much more widely than they are. As it is, although most shooting men are tempted to try them out at some time or another, and although they give rise to a good deal of hilarity on days in the field, they are expensive and misleading. Far better to learn to see shot in the air.

As you cannot do it for yourself, you need the observer to spot for you; and, incidentally, your own shooting will be improved by spotting, in turn, for him.

The observer should stand behind your right shoulder with his eye level set about three inches above the gun muzzle. He must search a point in the air on the line of shot and forward of the gun. If he looks at you or the gun, he will not see anything.

To begin with, it is sometimes a help if the observer stands on something like a soapbox for better elevation. But, with practice, it isn't necessary. If either or both of you are skeptical, you may find that it is a help to make a practical experiment.

Choose a safe level place in which you can fire from a kneeling position at a double spread of one of the larger newspapers. Start from a range of 15 yards, and increase it shot by shot to 40 yards. Your observer should be a foot or two behind your shoulder, staring at the target just over the line of the muzzles of the gun.

If you regret the apparent waste of cartridges, I promise you that what you learn from the experiment will save you many more in otherwise wasted shots in the field. From the shot-holes in the sheets of newspapers you can read how your gun is patterning at different ranges. You can accustom yourself to estimating ranges correctly; and how shot, like water out of a garden hose, spreads wider every yard that it leaves the gun.

But the chief purpose of the test is to help your observer to train his eyes.

Unless he is a very quick learner, it is unlikely that he will see any sign of the turbulence in the air made by the shot charge for the first twenty-five rounds. At fifty, if he concentrates, he ought to be seeing things.

If he isn't, it may be that he is suffering from what Robert Churchill called "observer's jump." What that means is that his concentration is diverted by the bang of your gun when you fire. You won't notice it yourself (or I hope you won't: remember the drill) because yours is the finger on the trigger. In your case, you are in the position of a man who can squeeze the mess out of a spot in his own body without any nervous reaction. But the observer is the man who has somebody else squeezing for him. Not knowing precisely when the pressure is coming, he jumps. It will help the timing of all parties if the observer signals the trapper to throw up a target by sounding a whistle.

So as a temporary measure, especially if the disturbance in the air is evasive, get your observer to plug his ears. In time, when the sound of gunshot becomes monotonous, he won't need ear-plugs. He will accept it like the background music on the radio.

As soon as your observer reports that, in static shooting,

he believes that he can see the flicker of a shadow, the ghost of the shot charge showing high or low on sheets of newspaper; and satisfies himself as well that the shot holes are more or less where he expected to find them, get on to flying targets.

Under a brilliant blue cloudless sky, he may be defeated. Under heavy cloud, he will find that he sees shot more clearly than he did in ground level shooting. If you both stick at it, he will surprise himself, and you, with what he sees.

Once your observer has learned to see shot—and you have learned how to see shot for him—straight shooting ceases to be guesswork. Soon, you will discover that there are flying targets—to begin with, the oncoming slow bird— you can bring down again and again. But don't delude yourself that that is good enough.

In the shooting school, when a man has his confidence and is getting a little above himself, the form is to ask the trap springer to "vary them." When you see clay pigeons coming from all directions, perhaps two or even four at a time, your shooting will soon be reduced to size. But it is tests like that which raise performance.

So when your observer is confident that he can see shot, get your trapper to "vary them." You will discover a whole heap of new shooting problems.

The professional shooting coaches look for a consistency of error. The difficult case is the man who is all over the place, never shooting with the same error twice. The explanation is often psychological, call it nerves, but it is always accompanied by bad discipline in the drill. For the rest of us, misses—once you know where you miss—are explicable.

After shooting with an observer for some time, you will even be able to explain your misses yourself. At first, the observer will be the one who tells you where you missed. With experience you will find that you can tell him not to tell you until you have made your own assessment of what you did wrong. Once you know what you do wrong you won't have to worry much about putting matters right on a day when you are off form.

You will find yourself saying: "I was behind that one because I poked, and I was trying too hard." "I was off-balance, when I took that one." "I missed him on the right because he curled." To make up for it, you will have those wonderful moments when you know, as your gun lifts, that you can count the target "dead."

Every shooting man has a pattern of temperament which can be conquered only with personal coaching. When your observer says, "You missed that crossing bird to the left" or "You were miles behind that tall one," I can only generalize what your problem is. But it cannot fail to help you to study some of the most common faults, and the causes.

ARE YOU MISSING BEHIND?

You are taking a second aim. You are hanging on the trigger. You are trying to meet the bird in the air by pointing at the air space in front of it. You are being thoughtful, instead of trusting your eyes and body movement to bring you unerringly, as they will, onto the target. You must point with your body, not your gun.

Make up your mind that you won't shoot at the target, but at a particular part of it. It doesn't matter whether you choose beak, wing, leg or tail, providing you glue your eyes to what you are shooting at. The pattern of shot will cover the lot. The important thing is that your eyes never leave the target.

Time your gun-mounting to shoot sooner than the moment when the shot looks easiest. Don't wait for it. Let fly, coming up behind, as soon as the target fills your eyes. Good shots kill their birds 10 yards sooner than average shots.

ARE YOU MISSING BIRDS ON YOUR LEFT OR ON YOUR RIGHT?

A right-handed man normally finds it easier to take a crossing bird moving from right to left than it is for him to take a crossing bird moving from left to right. The reason is simply that the body movement in taking the right-to-left bird comes naturally. The swing in the reverse direction is more difficult.

The solution is not to try too hard on a right-to-left bird. If your body-movement is sound, it is as easy as an oncoming one. Increase your determination when you tackle a left-to-right bird. In fact, it will mean that your gun-swing is quicker. Don't think about it. Just grit your teeth, and have at him. Rely on your eyes to carry your gun through. The answer is that you have just got to force your gun-mounting a fraction quicker.

ARE YOU MISSING OVER YOUR SHOULDER?

It is almost certainly the consequence of bad footwork. Men who miss in front often pull off showy shots behind. They shoot straight because they don't wait to think about it. In desperation, they make a clean swing, and kill. It is far better to shoot well in front. But you can learn from the lucky kills behind. If you miss, study the drill on feet.

ARE YOU MISSING GROUND GAME?

You are shooting too much from your own height. Your whole weight should be canted forward on your legs so that, when the butt of the gun touches your shoulder, you are aligned between the ears of your target.

ARE YOU MISSING IN FRONT?

An uncommon error. It could be that the stock of your

gun is far too short for you, so that the barrels are up before you complete mounting. You will be a rare bird if this is your consistent fault.

ARE YOU MISSING TO LEFT OR RIGHT OF TARGET?

It is probable that the cast in the stock of your gun is too much one way or the other off your eye level. It may be that you are canting the barrels as you lift them. Make sure that, when you mount, it is a level lift. If that is not the fault, your gun needs refitting.

ARE YOU MISSING BELOW?

You are possibly mounting the butt before the barrels. The butt could be short for you. It is also likely that a rearrangement of your grip will help. Try lengthening your hold—a handgrip you can slip on will be an advantage—on the fore-end. Best by far is to have your stock lengthened.

ARE YOU MISSING ABOVE?

Rare, like shooting in front. It is more likely to happen shooting at birds on your left and right. You are off-balance, and you throw your gun high. You have got your eye on the bird.

Whether you practice on clay pigeons or beer cans, and however efficient you become at it, there is still a world of difference between shooting "cold" and the performance you put up in the heat of actual field conditions. In the first place, an inanimate target is calculable; starting fast, slowing, hesitating and falling. Live game starts slowly, increases speed, and is unpredictable in behavior. So under field conditions, will you be.

8
KNOW-HOW
IN THE FIELD

The immediate aims in the field, after the indispensable preparation of dry practice and shooting at inanimate targets, are (1) the acquisition of constant (but relaxed) readiness; (2) the calculation of ranges; (3) the conquest of the nervous trait of trying too hard.

Whatever you are shooting at, from pheasants to spiraling woodcock, you won't do credit to yourself until you are collected within yourself. Knowing yourself, controlling your impulses, recognizing what you do wrong, are three parts of the know-how in the discipline of the field.

READINESS

A lack of readiness is, in shooting, no vice. In ball games and in all sport, except perhaps fishing, eagerness is a virtue. In shooting, over-eagerness is often objectionable, and it can easily become a dangerous habit. I remember shooting pheasants beside a well-known shortstop who, every time a bird came in sight, slung his gun as if he were

Figure 12. WRONG: The "natural" way of carrying a gun at the walk is the dangerous way. With every step, the barrels are swinging into the line of the man who is probably walking beside you. Even if you believe that you are alone, the fact is that, in crowded country, you are never alone.

snatching a hot ground ball. He was safe enough, but he was stealing the shooting from the guns on both sides of him. The rule is to offer the courtesy of the shot that's wide for you (unless previously agreed) to the man on either side.

Readiness doesn't mean that in a party, you are the one man with a loaded gun when everyone else's is empty. Recollect the case of the unfortunate fellow who was so eager that he put a cocked and loaded gun on the back seat of his car. He pulled it out by the muzzle, and shot himself dead in the stomach. There is an essential difference between readiness and over-eagerness.

Never mind if you occasionally miss because your safety has been left on. Never mind that you missed a chance because you fumbled when you were reloading. Never be ashamed that your gun was empty when somebody else pulled off a difficult shot. There's always another bird, and if you put safety first, another day. But, when the game is on, you can do a lot to improve your own performance.

At this juncture, I suppose I ought to tell you that your safety catch should never be pushed forward until the moment when your gun is mounting to your shoulder to shoot. That is the classic style. In practice, I can only say that I have known very few shots who have mastered the habit. Most of the shooting men I have come across take the greatest care to hold their guns in a safe position

Figure 13. RIGHT: The "unnatural" way is the right way. As you walk, push your gun across your chest so that the barrels are pointing straight in front of you. It is good practice to cant the barrels slightly upward. You will find that when the chance shows of a shot, you come much more fluently and accurately onto the mark.

against the possibility of an accidental discharge, but prefer to keep their weapons cocked in readiness for the chance of a shot. Personally, I have never doubted that the extra movement required to release the safety catch is a deterrent to smooth gun-mounting.

If you constantly carry your arm at a safe angle, you need not in my view concern yourself with the catch. Anyhow, it is an untrustworthy safety device. Better by far to take out the shotshells and carry your gun, broken and empty, when you are not expecting shooting. When you are in the ready position, it is reasonable to slip forward the catch. You protect your trigger guard, up to the instant of firing, with your extended trigger finger.

Use the catch, but don't make a fetish of it. You will find that you are less likely to be caught at an unready moment.

More shots are missed, not because safety catches are not taken off, but because so few shooting men take the trouble to give attention to quick reloading. In a hot corner, it is a useful accomplishment, well worth practicing.

First, make sure that you are opening your gun correctly. With doubles, for example, release the top lever, your first finger should be knurled over the right lock plate. With your thumb on the lever, squeeze both the lock plate and lever together. The pressure will be sufficient to release the stiffest lever you're likely to come across.

To open the breech, hold the stock under your arm with the barrels canted slightly sideways. This gives extra body leverage to assist smooth and easy opening. Draw down the barrels with your left hand, while the stock is still gripped between your right side and right forearm. Don't try to do it with your right hand, which should now be leaving the lever to reach your pocket or your belt for live rounds (assuming, of course, that you are using a gun with automatic ejectors).

If you are carrying out the operation successfully, your barrels will drop to an angle of approximately 45 degrees to the stock under your arm. The gun, turned slightly sideways, will eject the expended cartridges away to the right, rather than over your right shoulder.

Whether you have your ammunition in a bag or in your pocket, give them a good shake before shooting. The weight of leadshot in the heads of the cartridges compared with their lighter bases, will encourage them to turn heads uppermost. The advantage is that, when your fingers close on them, it is long odds that they will have settled in the best position for quick handling.

If you have only fired one shot, reloading a single chamber of a double-barrelled gun is a quick process. Where you are likely to be found out is when you have fired both barrels. It is a fact that the majority of shooting men make a double job of it. If there's no hurry, it couldn't matter less. But, in game shooting, it is always wise to assume that the best chance of the day will show at the moment when you are least prepared.

Quick loading yields far better results than snatched shooting. I used to know a great shot who had polished reloading to such precision that, when he was shooting, he carried a third shotshell by the brass between his first and second right fingers. He reckoned that, if he had put up three birds, he had time to reload one barrel and shoot all three. He often achieved it.

While a perfection of movement and timing like that is beyond most of us, it is still worth striving for. The art of slipping shotshells like oil into the chambers of a gun is a requisite of cool and unhurried shooting.

Try this: When you break your gun, your hand should be travelling toward the unfired shotshells. If you have shaken them, they should come to your fingers easily, brass up. As you collect them, make a movement so that one shell is more prominent in your hand than the top one by about three-quarters of an inch; in other words, pick up the two shells in an over-and-under position. Insert the nose of the higher shell into the right barrel, but don't let go of it. Using it as an axis, twist your wrist so that the other shell turns over the left barrel. Then let them both go.

On paper, it may seem a laborious business. But, if you take the trouble to master the twist, you will gain a reputation for the speed in which you reload.

Don't allow speed to relax your safety precautions. There is always the risk that once the cartridges are home, you will lift the barrels to the stock of the gun instead of the stock to the barrels. When you ejected the spent cartridges, remember, the stock of the gun was tucked under your arm. Keep it there. Close the gun with a pressure of your right hand, with a slight forward inclination of your body. Some men favor a lift with the forearm under the stock to close the gun. Take your choice.

You are right, whatever your personal style, if the muzzles of your gun remain inclined, in reloading, toward the ground.

THE CALCULATION OF RANGES

You will more often let a chance pass, within easy range of your gun, than take a shot which is outside the potential of your weapon. This is not what is usually said in books about shooting. With the admirable object of preventing sportsmen from wounding without killing at long ranges, the emphasis is usually the other way.

In most shotgun work, the common fault is to exaggerate distances. If a pheasant or a partridge fills your eye, it is very unlikely indeed that the bird is out of range. The fact that you think it is too far is quite likely why you take second aim, and miss.

At ground level, most of us have mental standards of distance. It may be the length of a miniature rifle range, or some other familiar unit of measurement. Against the sky, height is far more difficult to calculate. Ducks that look as high as the clouds are often within reasonable range. Again and again, shooting men congratulate each other on shots which, in truth, never extended the gun.

It's a good policy in the field to practice gauging distances. If you are standing 40 yards away from a belt of trees, for example, and the trees are 10 yards high, the extreme distance when a bird tops the trees will be about 45 yards. And you will be more likely to overestimate the range than otherwise.

Robert Churchill was fond of saying that the time to shoot is when the bird "looks big enough to eat." It suited his way of timing the instant to shoot, but it may not suit you. In good light conditions, it is a fair rule for some people to say shoot when you see the eyes of an oncoming partridge, or the color of a pheasant. In bad light, if you wait for that, you won't shoot at all. Best of all, when you are looking for the chance of a shot, cultivate the habit of measuring instinctively the distance between yourself and a hedge, fence or haystack. When you believe that you have pulled off a very long ground shot, pace out the actual distance. You will be surprised, although I won't, how easily an estimated 40 yards turns out to be 20, and less.

A duck blind is the ideal place to accustom yourself to estimating distances. You are posted at a fixed point. You are likely to be shooting at all angles, and you have the opportunity of planting your decoys at paced ranges.

In inland shooting, the only game of the chase which you are likely to think is nearer to you than it actually is is the hare. Because the hare is the largest, estimates of range can be painfully misleading. Theoretically, hares are usually so easy that a reasonable shot should never miss them. In fact, they are missed again and again through miscalculations of distance because of the hare's size.

In the field, you will inevitably watch other hunters. Afterwards you will be listening to them.

In the first place, you may well find good shots who don't seem to do anything that I have recommended to you in this book. Next, if you ask them how they get there without the drill, they will look at you with blank faces. They just do it. A lot of gamekeepers are like that. They use a gun as if it were a third arm, untidily to the eye, but with an effective technique of their own. It often comes off among men who are raised in green places. But I can't recommend it.

Don't be deceived by men who can shoot the tip off a cigarette, who claim that you can either do it, or you can't. You can do it, too. If you cultivate style, you can become the sort of shot who looks classic, even when you miss. And you won't miss nearly so often.

In the shooting field, you will hear all manner of claims, about shooting performance. You can disbelieve most of them. I have seen a man shoot two driven partridges in front, change guns and shoot two behind, about three times in my life. I think—I am not sure—that I have seen a man with three dead pheasants in the air.

In your case, discount any claim—it doesn't matter anyhow—of shooting proficiency. You will hear people say that they have killed 75 per cent of the pheasants they have shot at. What they don't tell you is how many rounds they have wasted getting them.

In all shooting, rich man's and poor man's shooting, he is a first-class shot who can show an average of 25 per cent kills to cartridges. Experienced shots can put up a better performance than that on inanimate targets. In the field, others will think that you are rather good if, when you wryly count up your expenditure of cartridges against your contribution to the bag, you have done as well as 20 per cent. At that percentage, you will have shot more than your share.

I recall a shoot in which, after the day was over, we were all asked to write down on a scrap of paper what we estimated we had killed. "When we learn the total bag," one of us said, "I'll bet I owe fifteen birds to the rest of you." He was the best shot among us; and sure enough, when the bag was declared, he was right.

People who boast about their shooting are seldom the best shots. Never talk about your own performance, however satisfied with yourself you may be, and don't count the birds you only think you hit. Other people don't miss much of the game.

9
KNOWING WHAT YOU DON'T DO

I would prefer, because my sole object is to make you shoot straight, to leave this chapter out. But, unfortunately, you will meet shooting men, still far too many of them, who will try to suborn you with tales of how you should lead a bird. You will meet the man who will tell you that, although he gave yards to a skein of wild geese, the one he killed was three behind the one he shot at. You will even hear that the way to pull down high pheasants is to start shooting before you see them. A favorite form of advice is that you ought to have led that bird you missed by such-and-such a number of yards.

Let's begin by demolishing the theory of lead, aim by calculation against aim by instinct. Ballisticians have worked out the figures.

The velocity of a standard 12-gauge shotshell, over varying ranges, is known. As a simple example, 40 mph is the average speed of a pheasant in full flight. From that, it can be computed that the gun muzzle movement necessary for lead at a crossing bird, so that the pheasant and shot charge meet at the same time, is:

> 1½ inches at 20 yards
> 1⅝ inches at 30 yards
> 1¾ inches at 40 yards

From this, one may calculate that in general terms, a slow bird needs only half the allowance of the fast one and the birds at 20 yards only require 40 per cent of the allowance theoretically necessary for the 40 yard bird. Even these figures only relate to the bird crossing at right angles. For a bird quartering at 45 degrees all figures have to be halved. The bird seen straight in front, unless it is climbing steeply, needs even less allowance; and, if a bird twists as you lift your gun, no calculation of lead is any good at all to you.

I could give you more tables. Enough that a measured lead for a bird crossing at 30 mph is approximately:

> 2½ feet at 20 yards
> 4 feet at 30 yards
> 6 feet at 40 yards

These figures, of course, are worked out on the basis of the time it takes for the charge to travel from the end of the gun muzzle. The man behind the gun should consider personal factors like the time it takes him to press the trigger, and he should also make allowance for the lag in his weapon while lock mechanism and primer are igniting the charge. If birds flew at a level speed, if we had range-finders, and provided that we didn't lose a fraction of time in pulling the trigger after making the mathematical calculation, lead might work. As it is, I hope that I have said enough to prove that the judgement of lead is beyond the capacity of the most expert shot.

Shooting men, who talk about the leads they give, are talking verbal nonsense. All systems of shooting at moving targets founded on leads are inherently unstable and unscientific. The good shots who talk that way don't practice what they preach; otherwise, they wouldn't be good shots. Bluntly, they simply don't know how to express in words what in fact they really do.

You need never concern yourself with lead; indeed, you will certainly miss if you distract yourself by bothering with arbitrary predictions. Anyhow, you are wasting effort because your eyes are the most beautiful calculating machine of all. Fix your eyes on the target, regulate your gun-mounting to suit the convenience of your sight, and the job of lead will automatically, and exactly, be done for you.

What happens is this: Shooting at a quickly moving target, your eyes move more quickly. Consequently, your body work is quicker. At a slow target, your gun-mounting is more deliberate. In fact, if you are shooting straight, your eyes are working out all the complex mathematical problems of interception.

It is true that the rate of lift in your gun-mounting, the confident trigger pull at the moment your shoulder thrusts into your gun, are essential concomitants to straight shooting. But the correct rate of lift is something you needn't even think about, subtle as the movement is, providing you fix your eyes unerringly on what you are shooting at.

Your eyes will tell you infallibly when to make the slow-quick and the slow-quickest lift of the gun.

When you miss, ask yourself: (1) Was I off balance on my legs? (2) Did I hesitate, through lack of confidence in myself, before I pressed the trigger? (3) Did my eyes wander off the target? (4) Above all, did I follow the advice of the damned fools who tell you to shoot at a patch of air in front?

10
THE CARE
OF GUNS

Did I say that it is never your gun's fault if you miss? It is, once in a long while. After missing a season or two I was alarmed how badly I shot. My guns had always fitted me like a Brooks Brothers suit. If I did not do something silly, when I recognized my mistakes, I expected to put up a reasonable performance. Humbly I went back to shooting school.

The coach showed me that I was shooting consistently to the right. When he advised me to fix my eyes on the left of the clay targets, I busted them again and again. What had happened over the years was that my eyes had changed. I was not the loose-limbed young fellow I was when the guns were fitted for me.

If I had been an Arab oil sheik, I would have ordered a new pair to replace the old ones. As it is, I have to be content to make a minor modification when I pick up the target. A young man, even with a gun which does not entirely suit him, can put up a reasonable show. Professional coaches in the shooting school can look down the cast of a gun, assess the length of the stock, and blind your eye at clay pigeons. As I know from experience they cannot do it in the unpredictable conditions in the field.

One of the curious things about shooting game, unlike almost any other sport, is that age is no barrier. Experience is what gives a man an advantage. I remember watching a senior citizen of eighty plus outshooting all of us. He was not worried any more. He did not care whether he missed. He had at least sixty years experience of gun-mounting and foot work. And he had looked at partridges flushing in his face before most of us were born. In his old age he did all the right things. He had muscle memory.

That great English novelist and playwright Eden Phil-potts wrote a splendid one-act play on the truth of it. He dramatized how an old poacher on his death bed settled a lifelong feud with his neighbor by shooting from his bed through the window one of his neighbor's tame pigeons; and then died happy. That also was muscle memory!

It is likely that the old poacher who shot his neighbor's pigeon was using a calamitous gas pipe which ought to have blown him up. Many gamekeepers, and poachers, do. I want you to be more careful.

It is probable that you should not worry about the weight of trigger pulls on your gun. Sensitive shots prefer 3 lbs. right trigger and 3¾ lbs. left trigger on a 12-gauge. As a rough guide the weight of the first or right trigger pull should be approximately one-half of the weight of the gun. A 6-lbs. pull on a 13-lbs. 8-gauge gun feels just as light as a 3-lbs. pull on a 12-gauge of 6½ lbs.; or as a 2½ lbs. pull on a 20-bore weighing 5 lbs.

It is just as well to forget all about it. If you are having trouble with your trigger pulls, you can probably overcome the problem fairly quickly by going back to the drill. Churchill wrote: "If you are having trouble with your trigger pulls, practice gun-mounting with a slightly relaxed grip. If you do that all the little troubles of varying pull will inevitably disappear. If you are throwing your shoulder forward and making your trigger pull with a rigid finger a light pull is not really necessary; and, in the interests of safety, a pull on the heavy side is even desirable."

What it all amounts to is that, if you care for your gun you must at regular intervals take it back to a gunsmith. Although you may believe that you have kept your weapon in excellent order it is surprising what little details may need attending to. The more care you take of your car the better you will drive it. The more care you take care of your gun the better you will use it. Guns need service like cars.

These are the sort of faults you may expect:

1. It is likely that, after constant use, the action needs tightening. Normally, a good double should not close on a cigarette paper. Daylight, between the barrels and breech action, after you close the gun, is at best putting an immoderate strain on it.

2. Shotgun barrels are sensitive to dents. If you knock a barrel you make a bruise in the metal which must be worked out. Otherwise the shot charge every time you fire will thin your barrels.

3. You may well dent your stock. Gunmakers can raise dents in the wood so that you will never know that you have damaged it.

Cleaning a gun is relatively easy. Even though you use noncorrosive ammunition, you should still run a cleaning rod through your barrels. You cannot get enough protection against rain.

You must dry and protect your gun against rust after shooting. If you are a waterfowler on salt-water bays and marshes—salt is the most terrible stuff—you must work over your weapon with oil again and again. You must always look under the blades of your triggers and put a trace of oil into them to keep them clean.

And I hope that, with regard to your gun, you put it

together properly. When you break one, taking off the fore-end, dropping the barrels off the stock, it is relatively easy. Putting a double-barreled gun together requires altogether greater care. So many people burr the metal of the action in their hurry to close it.

Mounting and dismounting a gun should be carried out as a drill. To dismount, remove the fore-end and place it forward of the barrel-loop. Grasping the fore-end over the barrel-loop, bend the breech of the gun and remove the barrels.

That is easy. How you can damage your weapon is putting it together again. When you assemble your gun, remove the fore-end, and present the barrels to the stock, the stock held under your arm at a full right angle. Release the slide of the action above the stock at full pressure. Hold the barrels at a right angle, and suck the action face into the gun. *Suck* is the word. If you are buying an old gun you may quickly discover how it has been treated by looking at the hinge of the action where the barrels join.

All that you may say has nothing to do with why we miss. It has everything to do with it. If you have a sensitive interest in your gun you are more than halfway to shooting straight. You are working yourself into the mood of making it a part of you, an extension of your own arm.

11

SECOND
THOUGHTS

SCHOOLS OF THOUGHT

The method of gunhandling I have advocated in this book is based on Robert Churchill's method of teaching gameshooting. It is important to mention that there is another school, which teaches that when you lift your gun to your shoulder you should run your left hand up the barrels beyond the fore-end of your gun until you are gripping just behind the bead.

King George V, who was a fine gameshot, used just that method. For those who are suited to it, it is a sound gun-mounting style. Churchill himself had no criticism. He simply said that he believed that most shots would do better using his method. Yet, just as there are some who shoot more effectively with one eye shut rather than with both eyes open, there are those who find it suits them to run the left hand up the barrel as they lift and swing. You may make your choice without any doubt that yours is still a classic style.

CHOICE OF SHOTGUN GAUGES

In the days of muzzleloaders a 14-gauge was the fashionable gun for game. It was roughly defined as a gun in which fourteen lead balls down the barrel weighted one pound. Today the most favored game gun is a 12-gauge. Without entering into technicalities, the modern 12-gauge is little different from the 14-gauge of our forebears. It has been established as the best gun for wing shooting.

If your gun is built for you, you can have it chambered for 3-inch ammunition for waterfowl. You can have the barrel full-choked. For hunting situations, if you shoot straight, you won't go far wrong if you ask for improved cylinder in the right barrel, modified choke in the left. You want a little tighter constriction in the shot charge for what may well be a longer shot when you fire the left.

It is an eclectic point. If you are on your target it won't make more than a fractional difference to the results you get. Still, if it gives you confidence, it is valuable.

BARREL LENGTHS

There has always been controversy about the advantages of one barrel length over another. Churchill had much to do with it. He insisted that his own guns, with 25-inch barrels, lifted more smoothly onto the target, and handled better, than the guns with 28-inch barrels.

It's an old argument. In the earlier part of the nineteenth century, the general notion was that the longer your barrels, the nearer they reached to the target, the better they were. Sportsmen shot with gun barrels of 32-inches and longer. By the middle-third of the century the fashionable length was 30-inches. By the turn of it, the length had been reduced to 28-inches, which is the most common length today.

I have shot Churchill's 25-inch guns all my shooting life. I am satisfied that much of what he argued is correct. I have also come to the conclusion that the 25-inch barrels, admirable as they are for quick shots in cover, are not necessarily the best guns for a tall long-necked man. They suited Churchill, who was a square short-necked one, admirably. He could take the snap of the discharge, sharper than the recoil of a longer barrelled gun, without discomfort. No doubt the lift of his guns is marvelous. You are on target almost before you know it. But temperamentally, the longer lift may well help another man better. It is up to you to decide what personally suits you best.

SHOT SIZES

I hope that you are not a shot size fanatic. In the old days before shot was properly milled, hopelessly irregular, it made a difference. Today it truthfully does not matter a damn whether you load your gun with No. 7, 6 or 5. If you swing your gun into the right place you will kill. Shot patterns from standard cartridges are as regular as the powder behind them. If you shoot straight you will kill a grouse as surely with No. 5 shot as you will with No. 7 or 8. Perhaps not quite as surely, but the difference in the pattern is really negligible. The punch of the shot, too.

Disagree with me if you like, But it has happened to me too often that I have killed snipe with No. 5 and pulled down a high mallard with No. 7. If you never use anything but No. 6 you won't fail to shoot dead anything you deserve.

SECONDHAND GUNS

With new guns as expensive as they now are it is tempting to buy a secondhand one. It is of course best to buy a secondhand gun from a reputable gundealer, who can modify it to see that it is a reasonable fit for you. It is more dangerous to buy a gun from an acquaintance who is sure to assure you that it is the hardest-hitting gun he has ever known. That is nonsense. A gun can only shoot as hard as the propellent in the cartridge sends it. The best it can do after that, providing the choke in the barrels has not been shot out, is to steady the charge on its way.

Even good gundealers, anxious to make a sale, may be understandably reluctant to tell you some of the things you should look for. Always break the gun into its essential components when examining it. If it's a double, there will be three components—fore-end, barrels, action. Begin by looking carefully at the metal where the barrels hinge onto the action. If the edge is bruised, you will know at once that it has been handled by someone who did not know how to respect it. Look down the barrels from both ends reflecting the light down them in search of pits. Good barrels should be bright.

Putting the gun together, see if you can find any light between the barrels and the action face. A nicely tightened gun should not close on a cigarette paper. Look for dents in the wood of the stock. Try the pull of the triggers on snapcaps.

The price you pay should depend on those essential factors.

DAMAGE

If you are blessed with your own guns don't delude yourself that they won't need regular attention. If you put them away in their leather case they will deteriorate as surely as a car that is never taken out of the garage.

If you use them a lot, you are liable to get dents in the barrels and the stock. Dents in the barrels are dangerous. If the dents are not worked out by a gunsmith, every shot you fire will put pressure on the spot and wear the metal away.

The repair of dents in the wood of stocks may be regarded as cosmetic. They are not essential to the efficiency of the gun. But if the mahoghany of the stock has a polish like an old piece of furniture, it does a power of good to the proud shooter who is handling it.

Nothing much, you may think, to help you when you miss. If you think that, you will be wrong. If you go out of your way to see that your gun is just right, you will be well on your way to being just right yourself.

APPENDIX

BORE DIAMETERS OF SHOTGUN GAUGES

10 Gauge	.775 Inch
12 Gauge	.730 Inch
16 Gauge	.670 Inch
20 Gauge	.615 Inch
28 Gauge	.550 Inch
410 Gauge	.410 Inch

SHOTGUN CHOKES AND PATTERN PERCENTAGES

CHOKE	PERCENTAGE OF SHOT IN 30-INCH CIRCLE AT 40 YD.
FULL CHOKE	70-80 PERCENT
IMPROVED MODIFIED	65-70 PERCENT
MODIFIED	55-65 PERCENT
QUARTER CHOKE	50-55 PERCENT
IMPROVED CYLINDER	45-50 PERCENT
SKEET NO. 2	50-60 PERCENT
SKEET NO. 1 (CYLINDER)	35-40 PERCENT

APPROXIMATE NUMBER OF PELLETS PER SHOTSHELL

OUNCES OF SHOT TO SHELL	NO. 00 BUCK	NO. 0 BUCK	NO. 1 BUCK	NO. 3 BUCK	NO. 4 BUCK	BB	2	4	5	6	7½	8	9
1⅞	15					93	168	252	318				
1⅝					41	81	146	219	276	366			
1½	12						135	203	256	337	525		
1⅜		12	16			69	124	186		309			
1¼					27	63	113	169	213	281	438	513	731
1³/₁₆								160					
1⅛	9		12				101	152	191	253	394	461	658
1				20			90	135	170	225	350	410	585
⅞								118	149	197		359	512
¾								101	128	169	263		439
½								68	85	113	175		293